meditations for kids
by kids

Jarrah, Tahnaya, Ky & Jessica Wynne

BLUE ANGEL GALLERY
AUSTRALIA

meditations for kids
by kids

This edition published in 2006 by

Blue Angel Gallery, Australia

80 Glen Tower Drive, Glen Waverley, Victoria, Australia 3150

Phone: 61 3 9574 7776

Fax: 61 3 9574 7772

E-mail: tonicarmine@optusnet.com.au

Website: www.tonicarminesalerno.com

Meditations and Paintings by Jessica, Ky, Tahnaya and Jarrah Wynne

Design by Kiddiepunk Graphics

Edited by Tanya Graham

Printed in China

ISBN: 0-9757683-6-0

DEDICATION

For Lynn & Chris,
our loving mother and father,
who we all really love.

MEDITATIONS FOR KIDS
by kids

CONTENTS

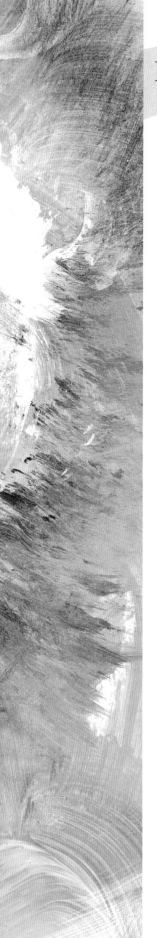

INTRODUCTION

JESSI WYNNE – AGE 11

Let me introduce myself. I am Jessi, sometimes known as Jessi - Jade, Jessica or Jess. I am very happy in my life and try to focus on the positives. I feel we are all on a journey in life no matter what paths we take. Welcome your own journey.

Even though I am eleven years old now, I wrote about half of my meditations when I was ten. Meditation for me is very important in my life as it brings peace and serenity to me. To get my balance for myself I meditate nearly every day and feel healthy and happy. I meditate when I have something difficult in my life that I need to work out, such as, sometimes when I am in an angry mood I meditate and I feel so much better afterwards. Meditation is a very peaceful thing to do. As well as relaxing your body it also relaxes your inner self, your soul. I am very joyful when I meditate. I suggest you meditate as often as you can.

Some of my interests are: singing, writing poetry, painting, reading long novels and having fun on our two and a half acre property. I also enjoy interacting with people of all ages. I love the beach and nature just so much; they trigger a sensation of freedom in me. The waves rolling on the beach symbolize to me each one of us rolling on our own path in life.

I feel so fortunate that I have the opportunity to be home educated because I get to learn around my family and learn in real life. Life is such a great curriculum. It's such a free way of life and it's so fun. It's really not that hard and we teach ourselves mostly, Mummy is just there guiding us. For my whole life I am learning and living in a truly natural, fun, meaningful way.

I encourage you to free yourself of any fears you have by opening up your soul and sharing it with the people that mean the most to you. It is really working for me.

Live your dreams, be positive, follow your own heart and you will enjoy your whole life. Live each day as if it was your last. Remember your little child within and keep that little child alive inside your heart, loving it for your whole life. Know you CAN do whatever you want to do in your life. Enjoy my meditations as they let you flow as freely as a bird upon the river of life.

KY WYNNE – AGE 9

Hello there! My name is Ky. I am a happy nine-year-old boy with a loving mummy and daddy that really care for me. I also have one brother Jarrah, and two sisters, Jessi and Tahnaya, that love me too. I enjoy my life, sending love out into the world, really living each moment.

I created my meditations for other people to enjoy as well as for myself. I love meditation because it makes me feel relaxed and it cleanses me. I wrote some of these meditations when I was eight as a gift for my daddy to help heal him. I continued to write more meditations to create this book so that others could also be healed.

The things I enjoy doing are: cooking everything and anything, riding my BMX bike, ball sports, playing with my dog in nature, writing, outdoor fun with my friends and being a 'little nipper' at the life saving club. The thing I like most though is cooking. When I grow up I really want to be a chef and own a tropical restaurant on the beach. It is fun being nine even though all ages are fun to me because I go through different changes along the way. My greatest feelings are love, peace and happiness. Don't fight. Love each other and you will feel good inside your heart. I want to share some of my inner thoughts which are: follow your instincts and let all the love into your heart and give some back into the world. I hope you use these in your life.

Travel with me through my meditations allowing yourself to be free as you float your imagination gently upon the clouds in the sky of your dreams.

TAHNAYA WYNNE – AGE 7

I am a happy person called Tahnaya which means spirit of the mountain lion. I have just turned seven but I wrote all of my meditations when I was six years old. I have two brothers who are fun to play with and one sister that is very kind to me. I have a great mummy and daddy who I really love.

I love meditations because they flow me in a peaceful direction through my life.

I would love you to journey with me in my meditations. I wrote these meditations to heal people, including myself. Maybe you would like to write some meditations yourself. It's very easy. All you have to do is find a quiet spot, relax and tell yourself you CAN do it. Let your mind be free.

Meditation and love and nature are what I do in life. Some things I love are: reading, playing with my family and friends, writing, playing ball and tennis, running, being a 'nipper', rollerblading, being at the beach, being in nature, homeschooling, playing with my dog, music and all of life.

My gift to you is, "Follow your heart and follow your dreams because it brings happiness to your life. Give peace and love out and it will come back to you." I would like to be your friend. I am a very happy girl with a bubble inside me. I am feeling very happy in my life because everybody loves me.

JARRAH WYNNE – AGE 4

I am Jarrah. I am a happy boy and everything is my favourite thing to do. I like eating the most though. I love animals and when I grow up I am going to be a zoologist with heaps of animals roaming free on my huge property.

You will like my meditations. You have to close your eyes in meditations to see the pictures in your mind. I think meditations are fun. They give you good energy. I want you to have fun in your life.

P R E L U D E
BY JESSI

Meditation is one extremely effective way to relax the body and mind. There are many ways to meditate. Although there is no right or wrong way, you do need to find the way that suits you. You can sit quietly or use the guided meditations provided in this book making adaptations to these to suit yourself. With the visualizations we have written here, you will get the most benefit if you relax and totally let yourself drift into this other world.

When meditating you can either sit somewhere comfortable or lie down, making sure it is quiet and peaceful. It doesn't matter which position you are in, as long as it is comfortable for you. It is important to turn the telephone off before meditating as this can disturb you.

Even though this book is written for children, adults can use it too and they will get just as much benefit from the meditations.

It is very important when reading meditations to another person, to speak in a calm, peaceful, slow voice, like the breath of the wind blowing gently upon the Earth, rustling the branches of the trees upon her peacefully. When you read these meditations, pause every so often to let the listener soak in what you have said. It is essential that you have your eyes closed so that you can visualize the picture in your head which allows you to be free with open thoughts.

When I meditate I like to lie down usually, but sometimes I sit up, it just depends on where I am meditating and how I am feeling.

When a problem arises or when you get stuck, caught in the nets of life or when your creative flow gets blocked, MEDITATE and you will find an answer. Your creative energy will flow again filling you up with a vibrant feeling. In this state, anything is possible!

These meditations are healing for your soul. With my two brothers and my sister, together we created these meditations because we found that we really benefited from meditating. We wanted to share meditation with others so that they could benefit from it like we have. It would be quite hard to imagine my life without meditation. I really love the fantastic feeling I get after meditating and what it brings to my life.

Meditation is very good for you, as it gives you a special knowing and inner peace with balance in your life. It relaxes your body while your mind floats along an imaginary river, trickling down the mountainside to emerge freely into the energy of the world.

*** ENJOY ***

THE MEDITATIONS

"This book will take you on a journey through the rivers and depths of the ocean to your inner self. It will open a channel of peacefulness and creativity inside you while you drift through the mountains and valleys, feeling as free as the wind blowing through your soul."

SILVERBACK

Close your eyes. Take a deep breath ... and let go. Take a few more deep breaths. Feel your body becoming more and more relaxed.

Imagine yourself walking down a beautiful path surrounded by blooming daffodils. Soon you come to a clearing which has a thick forest of woods around it. One tree in particular, a big old one, seems to be beckoning for you to come closer. When you walk over she whispers in your ear. "I am a very special tree, you can let go of all your fears, all you have to do is send them up to my leaves," says the big old tree to you. Send your troubles up to this tree. Let them all go.

You are now back on the path again and you are coming up to a large, old gate. This gate leads to your very own special place. You can do whatever you like in here. There are many wild animals, but don't worry, they are all very friendly. In this special land, there is always peace and no fighting. When you walk in the gate, you feel just like all of the animals, with peace in your heart and not wanting to hurt each other.

In your garden is a forest of trees, and as you make your way through them, you appreciate the prettiness of the area.

Soon, you appear in a clearing. Around you are many big gulls, and they are sitting rather still, as if waiting for something. When you enter, the largest of the gulls (he seems to be the leader) comes up to you and he tells you his name is Brimbe feather. He asks if you would like to ride on his back. You say, "Yes, I'd love to."

As you get on his back you feel excited. Soon you are flying across the oceans to a tropical beach where he lands. Then he flies back over the oceans and leaves you all alone.

Feel the magical air around you. Let your inner strength comfort you. It is okay to be on your own sometimes. You are very safe and loved.

You decide to go for a swim and stripping off your clothes, you jump right in. Feel the cool water rushing past your body as you swim along.

Suddenly, you feel something nudge you from underneath. It is smooth and gentle. Then a fin appears. You look up and, "Oh, how lovely, it's a playful dolphin!"

He is asking if you would like to have a ride on his back. Without thinking, you quickly say, "Yes."

Down, down, down you go, through the deep, dark water, into the depths of the ocean. Feel yourself going deeper down into your own inner ocean.

Finally the dolphin, whose name is Silverback, stops at a small crack in the seabed. He swims inside and there is his family. The mother, with her four little babies: Duom, Liddy, Miram and Shores. Their mother's name is Able.

As you are admiring them, one of the babies, Shores, swims up to you. You giggle and pet him. Already you are in love with Shores. They are all very cute and seem to radiate a beautiful energy out of them. Feel the energy of the baby dolphins enter your soul. Feel your body being soaked in love.

Have fun with the four baby dolphins. Soak in their energy. Feel the love around you. You are loved. You are very safe.

JESSI

THE HEALING CANDLE

You have decided to visit your special place, your own unique place, your garden. Let your body relax. Any thoughts that pass through your mind, let them go.

It is a bright sunny morning at the edge of your garden. The sun has just come up and you feel something very special about today, but you don't know what it is.

You pass the wise old troubles tree on the way to your garden. Let all your worries drift up to this tree. As you do so you feel your guardian angel wrap her warm feathery wings around you. You are safe.

Next you go and open your shiny green gate that leads to your garden and it squeaks noisily. You shut the gate behind you.

You seem to be drawn oddly to an old, old gum tree. When you get there you notice that it has a hollow in its trunk. To your sudden surprise out of the hollow pops a grey and white ringtail possum. He is very friendly and you talk for a while but soon you get tired of talking and decide to travel further into your luscious garden. You say goodbye to the possum and set on your way.

You walk for a while enjoying the lovely smells of the flowers and the sounds of the birds. There are so many: parrots, cockatoos, white-faced herons, ibises and lots more that you can not identify. You keep walking and after a while the tree-lined path seems to be getting wider. After a couple of minutes you reach a small clearing adjacent to a babbling brook.

At the edge of the clearing is a quaint little house with a thatched roof and big oak door. You go and knock on the big oak door and a kind-looking pixie and his wife answer the door. They invite you in for a piece of freshly baked carrot and apple cake and cup of peppermint tea. You instantly agree because all that walking has made you very tired.

As you are eating the delicious cake you notice a very bright yellow and green light not very far away. You decide to go and see what it is. You thank the kind pixies and head towards the bright light.

After a couple of very long minutes of walking you reach a ring of toadstools and in the middle is a very special white candle. You step into the circle and you know that you have this healing white candle deep inside you. Let the light of the candle flow through you. Feel its radiating light flow through you. You are so very loved by everyone. Let your inner light radiate out into the world. The light of your inner candle is love. Let it shine.

K Y

YOUR HEALING POWER

Take a deep breath and relax. Now close your eyes. You feel so peaceful when your eyes are closed. Let all worries and fears drift away. There is no need to get worried. Your guardian angel is with you and will always be with you, protecting and loving you.

Let all sadness, guilt and anger drift into the past. Let it go. You don't want to take those negative thoughts around with you; they just eat away inside you. There is no use drowning in the sea of negativity, why not fly in the sky of positive energy, allowing yourself to drift freely in the wind. You feel a lot freer when you do.

Let all healing energy flood through your soul. Feel the energy drifting throughout your body, cleansing it like the rain washing over the trees. You may have some disease or sickness but you CAN heal yourself with the power of your magical mind. You only have to know that you CAN do it! You have to have trust in yourself. Let all peaceful thoughts flow around you, release all negative ones. You are loved by everyone.

Bless your life, enjoy it while you have it, you never know what is going to happen anywhere further than where you are now. Live each moment as if it was your last. Enjoy the presence of this moment, right now.

Let all love and healing power flood through you. Feel it like a stream flowing over the pebbles of the river. You are always safe. Let the lightning of your spirit heal you.

K Y

W I L D   W I L L Y

Close your eyes. Take a nice deep breath and relax. You have a golden moon inside you. This golden moon has love and white light inside it which fills your soul with shining, bright light. Feel the warm energy from your moon.

Take another deep breath and feel the peaceful energy now that you are in your lush, colourful, healthy garden. Right in front of you, you see a pure white flower. Give all your worries or fears to this magnificent, sparkling flower. This flower is your worry flower. Take another deep breath as you release your worries and fears. You love the feeling of being free.

On your way across the rolling hills you discover a magnificent palomino horse. Instantly, you get a feeling of peace inside you. She looks at you as though she is trying to tell you that she wants to be your special friend. This is WILD WILLY. You can tell her anything you want to. She will understand you. She seems to know how you are feeling just by listening to you. Call her name, "WILD WILLY...WILD WILLY..." Instantly she gallops over to you like the spirit of the wind.

When she reaches you, you gently ask if you can have a ride on her lovely, golden back. She answers, "Yes, I would love you to." So you jump on her soft back and ride away together over the rolling hills. Feel the wind through your hair as you ride in the moonlight. Wild Willy's mane blows in the soft breeze. You feel very happy.

Take another deep breath as you look into Wild Willy's eyes. You know she feels your wonderful energy and you feel hers beneath you. Know that she will always be there for you.

Explore with your lovely, soft palomino, Wild Willy. Feel the nature through your hair. You are safe. Know that Wild Willy will come whenever you call her. You just have to call, "WILD WILLY... WILD WILLY..."

TAHNAYA

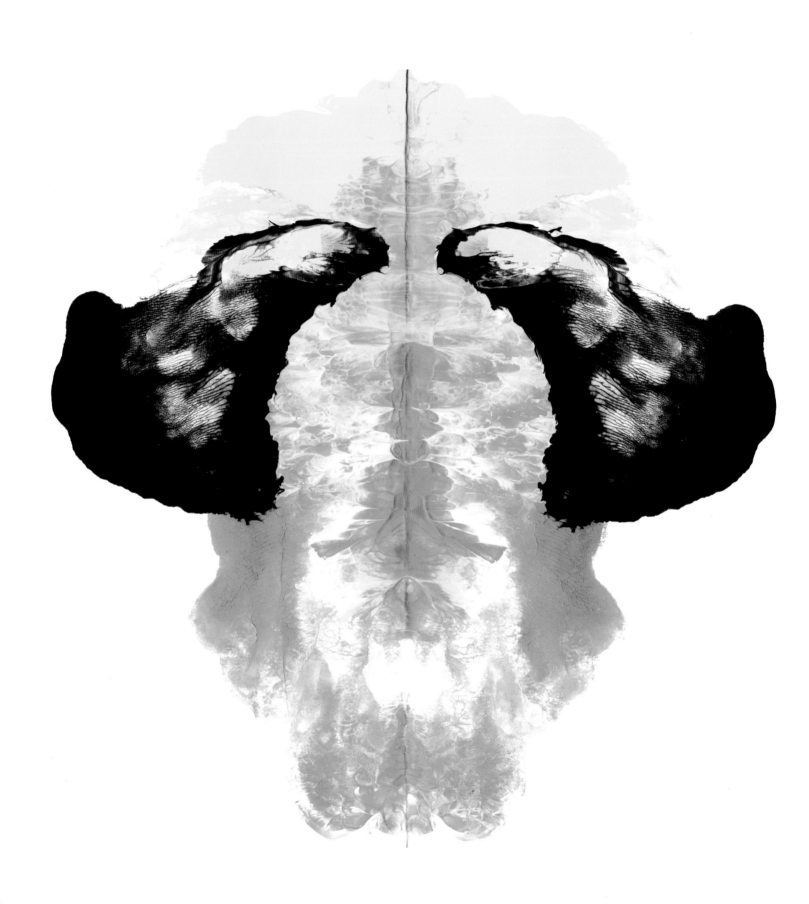

RELEASING

Close your eyes. Take a nice, long breath ... and let go. Take a few deep breaths, and as you do so let go of all the tension in your body.

Imagine a healing energy surrounding your body. This energy relaxes your body and gives it lots of love. Anything that is bothering you at the moment isn't doing your mind any good worrying about it, so release the need to worry about things. Take a deep breath ... and let them go. In your life, if you have any secrets inside you, let go of them. It isn't necessary to keep big secrets; they just eat away at your soul. Release them now.

To always feel peaceful around people, surround yourself with love, and always send love to others around you. Take a deep breath as you do this now. When you give out love, love always comes back to you, many times bigger. Feel the love coming back to you and feel it growing. With love in your heart you can not go wrong, no matter what happens. Take a deep breath as you send love to somebody, it could be anyone at all. Feel your body tingling with love. Just be in your lovely space. Feel the love in your heart. You are much loved.

JESSI

CRYSTAL CAVES

Close your eyes. Feel your head sinking into the pillow and let your body relax. Take a deep breath and let go.

Feel your whole self flowing down into the rivers and valleys, through the mountains of inner knowing and out into the depths of the ocean ... your soul. You ARE the cleansing water drifting through these mystical pathways. Feel the ripples flow through you. Let your mind be free.

Your body flips and flops as it flows freely over the many different channels inside you. Which pathway is calling to you? Take that path. Release the need to know where this path will take you. Feel the peace inside you as you go wherever this path leads. Know that you are safe. Just let it flow, and trust! Everything will work out exactly as it is meant to. Release the need to control anything.

You trickle slowly along your path, soaking in the beautiful energy around you. Along the way animals come to drink from you. Let them drink in some of your energy; you are always receiving more healing and loving energy from everything around you. Feel your light bubble within you. Allow all the magical energy from all of life around you to drift into you, filling you up and nurturing your inner soul.

Entering a large cave you are overwhelmed by the sparkling of the crystals shimmering into the cleansing water of your soul. Allow the energy of the crystals to drift into you. Feel the cleansing and healing energy enter your mind. You feel relaxed, peaceful, calm, joyful, cleansed and healed. These are the crystal caves of cleansing and healing.

It is the most special place in the world. You can come here any time you want to. All you have to do is close your eyes, take a deep breath and let go as you allow yourself to drift within the magical water that will flow you to these beautiful crystal caves.

Take another deep breath. Feel the happiness, peace and wholeness inside you. Floating further along your river bed you release your body while your mind floats along an imaginary river, trickling down the mountainside to emerge freely into the energy of the world.

Take these magical feelings with you out into your life. You are healed. You feel wonderful. You are a healer. Know that you ARE that cleansing water drifting through the mystical pathways of life.

When you are ready, slowly open your eyes. Notice your surroundings. Soak in the energy from around you and let it flood through you, shedding its light upon the world. Remember, you ARE a healer. Let your inner moon ... SHINE.

JESSI

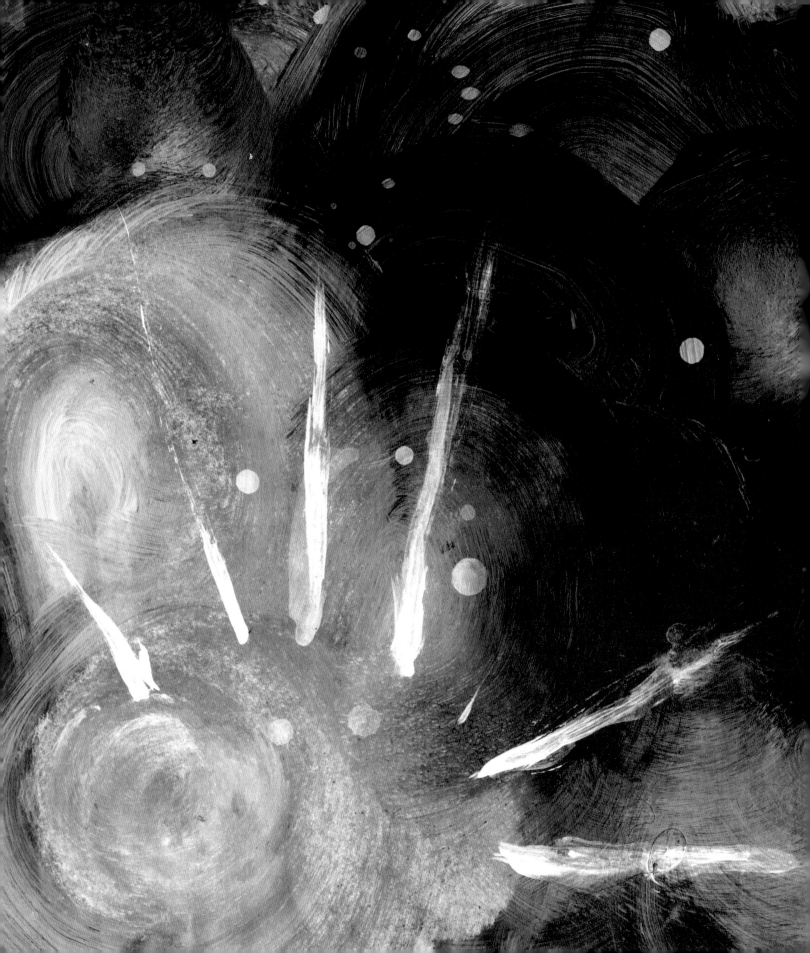

MIDNIGHT

Take a deep breath ... and let go. Now gently close your eyes and relax. Feel your healing candle above your head. Feel its light flow through your body like the wind through your hair. You are safe now and always.

Imagine yourself walking along a grassy track with some ferns dotted here and there. You see a large fear pool ahead of you shimmering in the moonlight. You can put all your fears in its waters allowing them to be released. Let all your fears drift into this pool. Feel the free sensation you have inside you now.

Just past this pond is a purple and blue gate. Go up to this gate and open it. Inside you feel a wonderful sense of love, peace and happiness. You know that you are in your garden, a peaceful place where there is never any hurting.

You hear some drumming ahead on the path and you decide to follow the sound. You soon notice that it is coming closer and in a small grassy clearing you see a gnome playing a tiny African drum. When he sees you he asks if you want to play a drum with him. You excitedly agree and he gives you a carved, wooden drum your size so you can play together. You enjoy playing for a while. Let the beat of the drum fill your soul. Follow your inner drumbeat in your life.

Soon you hear a strange animal noise even louder than the drum playing. You thank the friendly gnome for the fun time you had and set off towards the noise.

It takes a couple of minutes of walking then you appear in a small tree-lined paddock. You are just in time to see a baby foal being born. What a wonderful experience. Isn't he beautiful! He is pitch black with a white stripe on his nose. Feel his love fill your heart like the sun filling up the sky with its light.

You ask the mother horse if you can have a hold of her newborn foal. She says she doesn't mind, so you lift him up and give him a cuddle. Soak in his beautiful warmth.

You ask the mother horse if she has named him yet. She says she hasn't and asks if you would like to name him. You eagerly say, "Yes" and decide to call him "Midnight." She thinks it is a great name and thanks you for your choice.

Draw in the loving energy Midnight has. You are safe. You are loved.

K Y

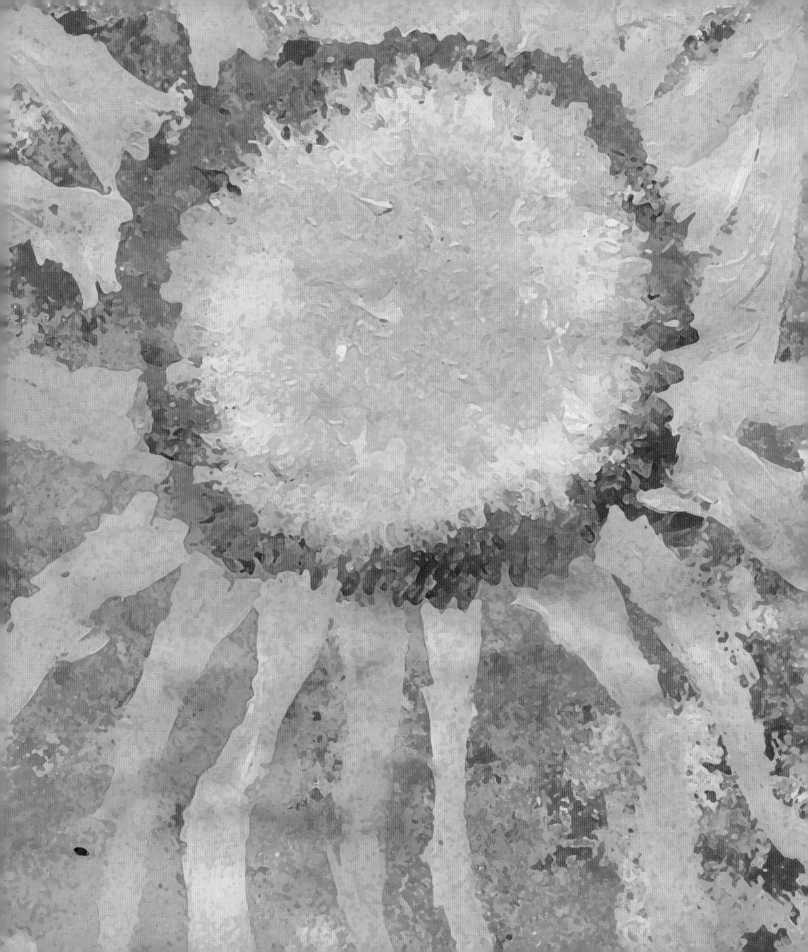

BLUEBERRY SMIGGLE

Close your eyes.   Take a deep breath ... and breathe out all of the tension in your body.   Take another deep breath and as you do so feel the energy rushing into your body. Breathe out all the sadness. Let it go.

As you walk along the beautiful path you come to a small clearing. The moment you sit down you sense that there is something strange happening, though you know that you will not become scared. The nearest tree seems to beckon you to come closer. She is a very old tree and she is asking you to release your anger and send it up to her leaves. This is Grandmother Sheoak. Release your anger now. Take a deep breath and let it go.

You feel very peaceful and calm now that you have got rid of all your anger. When you carry it around with you it only gets bigger and makes you feel sad.

You are now drifting along the beautiful path again. Look, what is that far away in the distance? You jog up to it and discover that it is a big, huge, wooden gate. This is the entrance to your very own magical garden where everything is always peaceful. Open the latch and step inside. Oh, how wonderfully peaceful you feel. This really is a beautiful place.

As you are starting to walk down the sandy path in your garden, you hear something far away.   It is getting slowly closer and you recognise the sound as the tinkling of bells. You are not afraid because you know that nothing harmful enters your special garden. You keep on walking along the sandy path and you hear the bells getting closer and closer. You decide to sit down for a rest because your legs are so tired of walking.

Just then, out of the corner of your eye, you see a very small sparkle. It is slowly getting closer and you turn your whole body around to look at it. Then you hear a small voice speaking to you through a miniscule microphone. It is saying, "We are fairies. Today we are having a party at Blueberry Smiggle. It is over the seas and far away. We want you to come with us."

Without thinking twice you quickly say, "Yes, I would love to, although how would I be able to get there, I have no wings?"

"That will be alright," the fairy says gently, and with a swish and flick of her wand you become smaller and smaller. Now that you are her size she gives you a pair of colourful fairy wings with intricate butterfly designs to wear. You are very excited.

It doesn't take long to fly over the seas and in no time at all you arrive at Blueberry Smiggle.
There is a party set out with such lovely foods. You meet many, many fairies who are all very kind and loving. You feel a deep sense of joy in your heart. Feel the love around you.

Explore with the fairies. Feel the wind which is gently blowing the trees' leaves above your head and know that the fairies are full of peace and magic, just like we are!! Feel the happiness and peace in your heart. You are safe. You are loved.

SPRING WIND
& WINTER MOON

Take a nice deep breath and relax. Close your eyes. You have your own star in your heart. It is your very own. Your star has white light and love in it. Take another deep breath. Feel the love from your star. As you do this you are going past your peace tree. Put all your worries on this magical tree. Take another deep breath, then go into your garden. You feel very peaceful without your worries.

Breathe in the mystical energy from your garden. It is your own garden. Have a look; there are three fairies and two pixies dancing in a circle. The fairies names are Autumn Wind, Spring Wind and SummerSage. The pixies names are Summer Sea and Winter Moon. You feel excited. You think a special something is going to happen.

Spring Wind and Winter Moon invite you to dance with them in the nice soft grass. Winter Moon says, "Would you like to change your name to Flower Blossom or Moon Dancer and be a fairy or a pixie with us?"

You answer, "Yes, I'd love to." So Spring Wind makes you smaller and smaller until you are as small as she is. They give you a purple and blue outfit with yellow and pink wings. As you put it on you feel much loved.

After you put the fairy outfit on, you dance with your new friends. Take another deep breath. You feel very happy dancing.

After dancing, you walk to a magical peach tree. You are there now. You see a hairy lioness sleeping under a tree. Go to her. She wakes up. She licks you. Go and hop on her golden back. She will take you on an enchanting ride. You feel the wind through your hair as she runs swiftly through the trees. Enjoy the ride.

When you want to wake up you can. Explore with the gentle lioness. You are loved. Feel the peaceful energy around you.

Tahndya

THE WISE OLD KOALA

Welcome to a wonderful, exciting experience. As you drift into this floating world, take some nice big deep breaths ... that's the way. Gently close your eyes. If you have any hurt or anger inside you, release it, you don't need that any more. Feel all the love in your heart as you let go of all your worries, you don't need them either. We are now coming to the entrance of a mystical world, your own special place, where no hurt ever enters.

As you enter you feel an energy surrounding your body and you become aware something strange is happening today, something you know will be exciting and fun. You make your way through the trees and you feel so happy right now. You notice the trees are starting to get thinner and less dense.

At this very moment, you walk out into a very peaceful, tranquil rainforest. There is a clearing with lots of trees surrounding an adorable trickling brook and beside that there is a small gathering of animals who are all talking together in low whispers excitedly. You decide to go quietly and see what they are doing. Take another deep breath ... and relax.

As you approach, one of the smaller rabbits spots you. You gently laugh, for this little rabbit is coming up to you, although he looks a little frightened. This has never happened to you before and you stop, sit down and watch, to see what will occur. All of the other animals are turning around to see what is happening. They were expecting you. They come up to you and all slowly begin to tell you that a wise old koala will be arriving soon and they would like YOU to meet him.

Eventually the wise old koala appears. He slowly sits down and calls you to him. When you are nearer to him, you notice how tired he looks, and you kindly ask him if he would like you to rub his head. He gladly agrees and he tells you his name is Limonso.

All of the animals have stopped their chattering to listen to this wise old creature. While you are rubbing his head he tells you about some of his adventures. He has all kinds of adventures, so you never know what you are going to hear about next.

Listen to his wonderful adventures and maybe, if you're lucky, travel with the wise old koala on one of his exciting journeys with him, throughout this mystical world. Feel the love. Listen to the river trickling through the rainforest and feel the essence of the river's love flooding through your body and soul.

JESSI

H E L P I N G

Close your eyes. Release all unwanted and negative energy; let it flow away into the past. Take a deep breath and as you do so, feel all the healing energy being drawn into your soul. Do this a couple more times as you feel the warmth of the energy cleansing your body.

It is the start of Spring and the trees, flowers and grasses are flourishing all around you. As you walk along the gravel path twisting into the trees, let all the nature around you soak in, mixed with the fragments of the brightly shining sun. You know that nothing can hurt you because you are in your garden, a safe and peaceful place.

Feel the love as you slowly walk along the path which is winding near a trickling stream. You are suddenly aware that you are being watched by an animal through the manna gum leaves. Release any fears you have inside you as you see a friendly wallaby bounce in your direction. He asks you for some help. You ask him, "What type of help are you needing?"

The wallaby answers, "All the animals are unsure of something and they need some help to get through it." You agree to help them because you have a great bond with the animals and a kind heart.

You follow the small wallaby to a clearing where lots of animals are sitting and waiting for you. They tell you about their wondering and fears and you tell them that they are all safe; there is no need to fear. You let them know that you will stay with them and find out what is unsettling them.

That evening when you are waiting with the animals you hear a CRASH! All the animals run and hide but you go and have a look and you see a grey and white koala sitting sadly in a pile of sticks and bark. You ask him why he is so sad and he says, "I have no friends because every time I fall out of my gum tree they all run and hide because I make such a terrible crash."

After reassuring the koala, you walk back to the clearing where you call all the animals over and tell them there is nothing to be frightened of. You explain to them it is only a lonely koala who wants some friends. All of the animals feel relieved and you lead them to the sad koala sitting in the sticks and bark. You introduce them to him and they become great friends instantly.

As for you, it is time to say goodbye to all your animal friends. You feel a great sense of achievement and have an incredible feeling of love inside you.

Close your eyes and drift along an imaginary river of energy back to where you belong. You are feeling an incredible amount of happiness because today you gave the lonely koala a friend. Feel all the love inside you. The more love you give out the more love you get back. You are always safe. You are very much loved.

K Y

K A N G A - P L A T Y

Lie down and relax and be floppy. Close your eyes. Which colour is your star? There's a big lot of energy inside your star. Have a deep breath.

Soon you come to a path but before you go on the path you have another deep breath. Soon you see the troubles tree. It's a big tree that you put your worries on. Once you've put your worries on, have another deep breath.

Then you walk along again. You come to your garden. You open your gate and it makes a clinking noise as you shut it. You get onto another path that leads to this big kangaroo ground. Then you see the mummy kanga and she has a tiny young joey in her pouch. You ask if you can have a hold of the joey. She lets you have a cuddle of the joey. It feels so nice, as nice as a pom-pom. Then you snuggle in the pouch of the mummy kanga with the little joey. Boing, boing ... she bounces you along. It feels as cuddly as a soft teddy bear.

Soon you come to a river where the platypuses are playing. The mother platypus lets you have a hold of the baby platypus she has just had. The baby plays with you in the water and you have a cuddle.

Soon you come to a tiny hole and you need your guardian angel's help. Your guardian angel makes you as teeny as an ant so you can get in the hole.

Soon you see the queen ant. She asks if you would like to help carry her eggs into the place where she stores the eggs with the other ants. Soon you say goodbye.

Next you climb up into a tree and meet the koala family. The mummy koala lets you have a hold of her baby koala. He feels so nice and cuddly. You can enjoy having a journey with the koala family in the manna gum trees.

Now when you want you can wake up. You are loved.

KY

THE KANGAROO

Close your eyes. Take a deep breath and make your body all floppy. As you do so, imagine a magnificent bright star. It is YOUR star. Your star is filled with love. Let the love from your star fill your body.

Take another DEEP breath. As you do so you are walking down a shaded path which leads you up a steep hill. As you walk further you eventually arrive at the problem tree. Take a deep breath and puff all your worries or scared thoughts onto this tree. You feel much happier now.

Now you enter your special garden. You are very tired so you lie down on some soft straw and fall fast asleep.

When you wake up you walk further into the trees. Take a deep breath and let go. You feel very peaceful.

After walking a bit further you find a red kangaroo which is eating some lush green grass. You ask, "Could I please have a ride to the Grandmother Wattle Blossom tree?"

The kangaroo answers in a low but soft voice, "Yes,

you can. Hop on my back." So he bounces you to your Grandmother Wattle Blossom tree, which has fresh green leaves. Take one more deep breath and let go.

You ask Grandmother Wattle Blossom if she knows how to help you. Listen to her as she answers your questions. You feel much happier now because she has answered some of your questions. You have a knowing in you that everything will be alright.

Then you go on the red kangaroo's back again to go home. His fur is very soft. He bounces happily through the forest.

You are safe and loved in your garden. Enjoy the loving journey home. You feel very peaceful. You are loved.

TAHNAYA

YOUR SPECIAL GARDEN

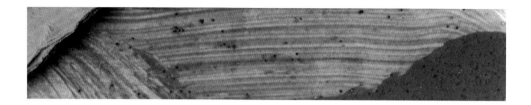

Imagine yourself walking along an old mountain trail. Take a deep breath, and as you exhale release all your fears knowing that you are safe.

You come up to an old green gate, you decide to open it. As you shut the gate you feel safe, because this is your garden. You feel your guardian angel wrap her warm silky wings around you, you truly feel safe in this special place.

You start to walk to a clearing a little while away and as you walk along you see a trail of ants. They ask you if you would like to come down to their ant hole and you say, "Yes, it will be exciting."

Your guardian angel makes you into an ant. Feel what it feels like to be an ant using your three pairs of legs as you follow the ant down his hole.

There are so many tunnels leading off the one you are on with ants scurrying in and out of other tunnels. You really want to go and explore them but the ant you are following keeps going.

He stops at an enormous room where a huge female ant is. She is the queen ant and she is laying hundreds of small white eggs. She asks if you want to help the other ants carry the eggs to a chamber. You would like to so you follow the other ants as you carry the eggs to the nursery chamber to be cared for.

Now that you have collected all the eggs, explore this big ant hole. Feel all the love as you relax. Let there be peace inside you. You are always safe.

KY

Y O U R   A D V E N T U R E

Make your body all floppy. Take a deep breath and relax. Close your eyes. You are now travelling along a winding path through the buttercup flowers. Skip along this path as you wonder what you will find at the end.

You discover that you are at the fear tree now, so let all your fears go. Take another deep breath. Now go into your garden.

You hear enchanting music as you enter your garden. It means there is a party at the Great Old Papa tree. Go over and join in the fun of dancing in a circle.

After enjoying the dance, you eat some little biscuits and cakes brought by some purple, pink and yellow fairies. You say, "Goodbye, thank you for the yummy biscuits and cakes," then you walk a bit further through the trees.

You see a golden beach with clear blue water. As you step onto the sand you feel the sand squish between your toes. You walk to the water's edge and start swimming through the warm water. You swim out deep to the dolphins and whales. One kind whale called Spots invites you to have a ride on her back. She jumps up and down in the warm waves. You feel so happy as you enjoy the exciting ride.

After your ride, Spots is going to give you to a dolphin called Splash to have a ride on her back. Splash takes you down deep into the clear blue ocean. Feel the love as you go deeper and deeper. Take another deep breath and let go.

After your ride on Splash she takes you back to the golden sand. You are very tired but happy.

You walk back past the Great Old Papa tree where the party was. You meet a beautiful, soft, tawny-coloured lioness. She is sleeping. Play with her. Jump on her back. She is very friendly and cuddly, she is your friend.

Explore with the soft lioness. You feel very peaceful. You know you are safe. Feel the love as you flow through nature. Take a deep breath and let go.

TAHNAYA

W O L F   L I O N

Close your eyes.   Be relaxing.   Now you go into your garden.   There's little foods in your garden.

A friendly wolf is waiting at the trouble tree for you. The wolf will eat all your worries up.   Take your worries out of your mouth and let them go to the wolf.

A lion is waiting in a field of flowers for you. The lion is friendly. When you walk to the lion, closer, you hear chattering going on.

It's getting night time. The lion will take you back to your house. He will walk or run. You are safe.

JARRAH

MRS. SNAKE

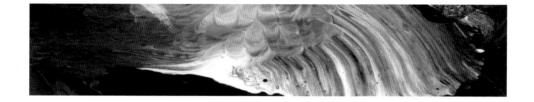

You are invited to a wonderful experience you will never forget. Slowly close your eyes. Take a deep breath ... and relax. Take a couple more deep breaths. Feel your body becoming more and more relaxed.

Imagine yourself walking down a sandy path. You glance over at a particularly beautiful tree and from behind it appears a palomino horse. She trots up to you and says, "I am a magical worry horse, all you need to do is give me a big hug, and as you do so, give all your worries to me. I will gallop to a special land where only I can go to release them." Somehow you understand her. Go and give her a big hug. Let go of all your worries. Take a deep breath and let them go. Without your worries you can be free to be whoever you want.

You are now back on the path and you meet your guardian angel. She is silvery white and she is always there, protecting you, guiding you. Whenever you are in a difficult situation, just ask her to help you take the right path and she will be right there beside you. Take another deep breath ... and feel your guardian angel with you.

She takes you to a gate which leads to your very own special place, where there is always peace and love. In this land, the animals speak your language, so you can understand them. Your guardian angel is opening the gate for you to walk inside. Next you say goodbye to your guardian angel and you watch as she fades away. But you know that she is still right there beside you.

When you step through the gate, you notice how quiet and still everything is. The only sound you can hear is the sound of the trees rustling.

Hang on ... what is that? It seems to be moving so you follow the sound for quite some time through lots of bushy shrubs until the sound stops quite suddenly and slithers out of the bushes. It's a beautiful, shimmering black snake! Although she may look scary, she is actually very friendly.

Next she says, "Hello, my name is Julia. I live in this forest with my husband and my seven little snakes. The sky is getting dark, would you like to come and have tea with my family?"

You reply after realizing that Julia is very kind, "Yes, I would love to, although I don't think I will be able to squeeze through your front door."

Just then, from thin air, your guardian angel appears. "I see you need me," she says and with a swish and flick of her hands you are shrinking smaller and smaller. Soon you are small enough to fit down Julia's door. You thank your guardian angel and say goodbye to her knowing that although you can't see her anymore she is still right there with you. You sense her energy.

As you walk into Julia's house, down many twisting tunnels, you finally arrive at the kitchen, where you meet her noisy family. There is her husband Boomer, and her seven kids, Lara and Tara, the twins, Sally, Dawn, Elaine, Spencer and Tom. They are all very kind and friendly. You sense the high energy flow in here and it is contagious.

Soon dinner is ready. You are all seated around a wooden table with ten chairs. Boomer serves frog balls, toad eyes, rabbit stew, chicken salad and lots more. When you have all filled yourselves with as much food as you can possibly eat, the food is taken away and dessert is served. Lamb meringue! You are given the first piece and it is huge. Oh boy, how yummy it is!

When you have finished eating you thank the black snakes for the lovely meal.

Finally, Boomer leads you through all the tunnels and when you are back out into the fresh air of your garden, you magically get bigger again. (I think your guardian angel's magic is working!)

On your way home, you think about all the lovely foods you ate at Julia and Boomer's place and you feel as if you have a lot of energy in you. You are happy to have some new friends. Feel the love inside you.

Walk the long way home through the trees. You are very safe. You are loved. Feel the peace around you and let it flow through your soul.

When you are ready, you can open your eyes, sit up and stretch. Notice your surroundings. Feel the beauty soak into you. Live the magic of the world.

jessi

BIRTHDAY SURPRISE

Close your eyes and relax. Take a deep breath as you let all the energy flow through you. Your garden is warm with the light from the sun as you walk along the thin gravel path twisting into the trees.

Have a look, there's a table and lots of chairs in a clearing near the Grandmother Manna Gum tree. As you walk closer you seem to see lots of dishes. Many animals fill up the chairs, all except one which is made out of gold and has your name on it.

As you go up to the table the animals sing "Happy Birthday" to you. When they have finished singing they invite you to sit down and eat. You do and you see to your astonishment that the table is laid out with fruit, party pies, sausage rolls, lollies and lots of other birthday surprises.

You enjoy eating all the party food and when you have finished, they all get together and start whispering to each other. Suddenly they all sing "Happy Birthday" again for it is your birthday today. Next, they give you a magical seat and they tell you that if you sit on it you can go anywhere you want to if you just say where.

Grandmother Manna Gum is beckoning you forward, she has a present for you too, so go and see what it is. Why, it is a little puppy, he is beautiful! You thank Grandmother Manna Gum.

As you are hugging the tree some pixies come up to you and start playing, "Happy birthday to you, happy birthday to you, happy birthday it's your special day." Then they rush up and give you a small basket and a balloon. When you say thank you, the pixies run shyly away.

You decide to go travelling on your magic chair that your friends have given you. You hug your cute baby puppy as you hop on your chair to begin your adventure.

Enjoy the rides as you fly through the sky. Feel the love and peace knowing that you can be whatever you want to be, and go wherever you want to go. You are free.

KY

THE PARTY & THE WOMBATS

Close your eyes. Take a deep breath ... and let go. Feel the peace in and around your body.

Imagine an energy flooding into your body. This beautiful energy heals any wounds that could have happened in your present or past lifetimes, it doesn't matter which. The energy also rids you of all your worries, which are harming to your mind. Let go of all your fears. Take a deep breath and let them go.

The winding path that you are walking on is streaking and curving up ahead of you.

You are now coming to a big, old gate that leads to a peaceful place. In this magical land you (or any of the animals you will find inside it) will not feel hurt. Open the gate and step inside.

The instant you do so, your body feels happy, peaceful, light and very different than it ever has before, all at the same time. Isn't the garden you are standing in at the moment beautiful? Take some time now to accept its beauty.

Listen, what is that sound coming from around the corner? You make your way to a path a few metres away. Oh, look! Just visible from behind a couple of big, bushy trees is an adorable sparkling stream, trickling down some dark coloured rocks. As you get closer, you notice a tawny barn owl perched upon one of the higher branches in a gum tree. When you get closer, he speaks to you. "If you follow that path down further into this garden you will come across a party in the woods. You are welcome to join the animals." You kindly thank the owl and continue down the twisting path.

Soon you hear a babble coming from a little further on. You keep on walking and in next to no time the trees that were surrounding the path stop to reveal a little party of animals, all chattering to each other and getting on so well together. Just as you start wondering what to do next, a little baby dingo crawls up to you and invites you to come and sit with his family. The party looks so fun that you agree. There are such lovely things that are set out for you to try. Meaty cakes, dewdrop drinks, dainty honey bites, frisky meringue and faltarta are just some of the foods you can taste.

When you have stuffed your body with all the lovely foods and drinks there are to try, have a rest under a shady gum tree for a while. Let your mind float above the tree tops.

During the time you are sitting under the tree, an old wombat approaches you. He is asking you if you would like to come back to his burrow to see his babies that have just come out of their mother's pouch. You say, "That would be so much fun."

As you go down the wombat's tunnel, into his burrow, take another deep breath … and relax. You are now stopping at the doorway of a large room. The wombat is taking you inside. Look at the baby wombats, they are just adorable. The mummy allows you to pat her babies. Let their love drift into you. Snuggle closer to the little ones. Feel your deep connection with them. They are animals, just like you are.

Have fun with the friendly wombats. Feel the peace and love around you. You are safe. You are much loved.

JESSI

L O V I N G

Close your eyes. Take a deep breath and relax your body. First relax your head and neck. Feel it tingling through your body. Next, relax your arms, stomach and legs; feel them sink into the bed. Take another deep breath as you let them go all floppy.

Feel the love well up inside you. Let it flood out into the world. As you send love and peace out into the world there is less chance of war. The more love you send out to others the more you will get back. Sending love out not only benefits others but also benefits you. Do this now. Feel all the love growing inside you when you do this.

Release the need to tease and hurt other people, it really only hurts yourself. You don't want it to eat away at you. Feel yourself letting go of all your anger and frustration, allowing it to flow away down the river towards the sea. Enjoy the free feeling you have inside you now.

You feel a lot better when you stand tall and free, loving yourself with the sense of peace inside you. When you have a negative thought, replace it with a positive one.

Feel worthy of yourself and trust other people, as well as letting other people trust you. Feel the love of life flood through your body. Let your inner soul shine. Let there be peace. You are loved.

KY

THE BROLGAS

Close your eyes. Breathe in the healing energy ... and let go
of all the negativity inside your body. Negativity brings your
energy level down lower and reduces your happiness. Take
another deep breath as you breathe in more healing energy.

Take some time now to let your mind peacefully and gently
drift over the different people in your life that aggravate
you ... think about what they do that irritates you
and send them love. We all need love and sometimes
we feel we don't get enough, so we lash out at people
and irritate them. Release the need to do this now.

Feel a moon floating around you. This is your very own special
moon. What colour is your moon? It could be blue, yellow,

red, orange, green, purple, white or any other colour at all. Let the light from your moon fill your body.

Feel the light flood into your head, through your neck and down into your arms, flowing down into your fingers and down into the very ends of your fingers. Feel the healing light flowing through your body. Feel the light going down your back and take another deep breath as you breathe out all the tension in your back. Feel the light going through your stomach, down into your hips, through your upper legs and into your knees. Let this light flow down into your lower legs, and into your ankles. Feel it flowing into your feet, until it reaches your toes, and feel the light flowing through your whole essence.

You are walking along a dusty path and as you do so, feel the wind gently blowing your hair. You walk along further and you come to a BIG, old tree. This is your problem tree. You can place all your fears and disappointments on this tree. Put your troubles on this tree. Take a deep breath and let them go. Feel the peace in your heart now that you have nothing to worry about.

As you keep walking along the twisting and turning path, you notice a greenly painted gate far away in the distance. You make your way to it peacefully and when you get nearer to the gate, you realize that this gate leads to your own special garden. In here everything is peaceful and there is always happiness.

When you step inside, you feel a feeling you have never felt before, a feeling of deep inner peace and happiness. Your garden is of such beauty that you never could have imagined. The flowers have such beautiful colours and textures that you pause and stare in wonder for a while. Then you start to walk down the tree-lined path in your garden.

Soon you come to a noisy swamp. There are a group of brolgas which are all dancing through the water. You walk closer to them and watch these mystical birds for a while. You wish you could be them, prancing and dancing about. Then, much to your surprise, you feel your body changing in shape and size. Within the minute this stops and you feel strangely different. Feel what it's like to be a brolga.

You walk easily across to the other brolgas and they are doing a special dance. Greeting them you ask if you can also dance. The other birds say, "Yes." You feel the beat of the dance within your soul. You watch their feet and you copy the other birds. After a while the brolgas stop dancing and they tell you that they are going to fly to a place somewhere up north, somewhere warmer. Then one of the older brolgas asks, "Would you like to come with us?"

"Oh yes," you answer. As you follow the other birds through the sky, take a deep breath. Feel what it's like to be flying up in the sky.

Enjoy flying with the brolgas. Feel the freeness of the air. Feel the magic. You are safe. You are loved.

JESSI

THE ADVENTURE
IN YOUR GARDEN

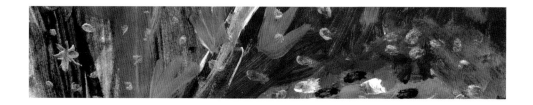

Take a deep breath and relax knowing that you are safe
as you enter your peace-scented garden. Love is around
you, the air is scented with the smell of the beautiful
flowers and the birds soar over the tall trees. In the bright
blue sky are parrots squawking loudly and kookaburras
laughing away while other birds are chattering to each other.

As you walk along the winding paths of your garden you see
little animals scurry through the undergrowth while bees
pollinate the flowers. You truly feel love in this special place.

The trees seem to want to tell you something, bending their
branches forward and whispering to each other in a tone
that you can not understand. You keep walking along and

ahead you see a clearing. As you walk up to it you notice an enormous lion. You go up and stroke him, feel his warmth. As you do so you see a bright green door in the great old tree. You decide to go and open the door but before you do, take another deep breath as you say goodbye to the lion. He answers in a deep voice, "Goodbye my friend."

As you turn the handle to the tree you take one last look at the magnificent lion then step inside. You see hundreds of staircases and even more doors.

You could go and have a look in some of the doors. As you walk up the nearest staircase you see an oddly-shaped door and open it. Inside you see a friendly squirrel and you make friends with him. You both decide to go and explore this tree. Discover the never-ending pathways of this house. Let the energy of the tree flow through you.

When you are ready you may want to stretch and yawn, then take a deep breath. Let the essence of peace flood through you. Enjoy this moment, have fun. You will always be loved.

K Y

THE SQUIRRELS

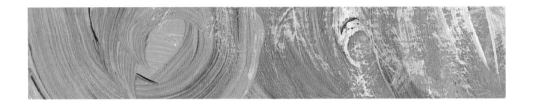

Feel the love around you. It is peaceful. Gently close your eyes. Take a couple of deep, relaxing breaths... and let go of all the tension in your body.

You are now coming to a lovely space beneath the trees and you make your way to a spot of healthy green grass and sit down. The air around you seems to be asking you to release all of your worries and they will be blown far away, never to be thought or felt by anyone. Take a deep breath and let them go. Doesn't your body feel good now that you don't have anything to worry about? Worrying about things only brings down your level of happiness and makes you feel sad.

You are now standing up and look, just over there is the entrance to the most peaceful and loveliest place you have ever seen. How about you go and have a look at it?

As you approach, you notice an old rusty gate. Open the latch and walk inside. As you do so, your body feels extremely happy and light. There seems to be a bluebell-lined path starting at the gate and you walk slowly along it until the path turns sharply and stops.

Just then you notice the beauty of the garden. There are a few gnarled oak trees in a half-circle which creates a lovely sitting area. Look around to see every type of flower and heaps of other pretty things that are not possible to explain. After no time at all you choose the prettiest spot of all. The most beautiful thing in the area is a circle of many different types of flowers, each with their own different look and scent. Breathe in the beauty of the flowers.

Now that you are seated on a comfortable piece of moss, you look across to another beautiful area and to your delight you spot a chestnut squirrel collecting acorns. He is coming up to you. When he finally reaches you, he tells you that he is a father squirrel and he has babies inside his little home. He is asking if you would like to come with him to see them.

You follow him down, down into his burrow. Then he shows you the baby squirrels. Aren't they cute? The mother squirrel allows you to have a hold. The two-day old baby squirrels are so small and cuddly. Feel the softness of their fur. Explore with the family of squirrels and have fun.

Love is around you. Feel the presence of the magic in this garden as you float through the mystical air. You are loved.

JESSI

Close your eyes. Take a deep breath and relax. You meet the peace tree. It is outside your garden. Put all your worries on this special tree. It accepts anything you put on it.

You go into your beautiful, relaxing garden. You see a magnificent fairy singer singing as you enter your garden.

You meet a brumby filly as you approach the Grandmother Eucalyptus Tree. Go and cuddle her as if she is yours. Go and ride her. You gallop and gallop through the forest. Your hair blows with the soft breeze.

You meet a black and white cow sleeping in a fairy clearing. She would like you to jump off the filly and jump onto her back. She will take you on a wonderful ride, to a river, to a waterfall and to a water fountain. Feel the joy inside you as you run swiftly among the trees.

Explore the nature in your garden with the happy and graceful cow. Feel the love in your garden. You are so safe. You are very loved by all the animals and all the people in your life. Let the love and light of nature fill your soul.

TAHNAYA

T H E   E M U S

Close your eyes. Take a deep breath ... and let go. Take another deep breath and as you do so breathe in positive energy. Release all the tension in your body. Let all of your negative energy drift out of your body to be swept away by the wind and carried to the mountains.

Imagine you are walking down a flower-lined path. The flowers have such wonderful colours. Breathe in their fragrance. You keep walking along and you come to a small clearing. Just over there is a large, old tree. This is your problem tree. You can put all your troubles on this tree. Place your fears on this tree. Take a deep breath ... and let go of all disturbing thoughts in your mind. Feel the calmness in your heart now that you don't have anything to worry about.

Feel a moon around your head. This is your very own special moon. What colour is your moon? It could be any colour at all. Let the light from your moon come into your head, flowing down into your upper arms. Feel the light flowing into your elbows, and feel it going down into your lower arms and into your hands. Now feel the light from your moon coming down into your fingers and bring the light down into the very ends of your fingers. Feel the awareness of your moon in your fingers. Take a deep breath ... and let go of any tension in your back. Let the light flow down into your spine. Bring the light from your moon into your stomach, feel it going down to your hips, into your upper legs. Feel the light going through your knees and into your lower legs. Bring the light from your moon into your feet, and down into your toes, down to the very ends of your toes. Feel the beautiful sensation through your body.

The instant you step foot in your garden, you feel the beautiful tranquillity. There are three tree-lined paths that lead left, right and straight ahead. Something seems to be telling you to go on one of the paths. Listen to your inner voice which will tell you which way to go.

Soon you hear a distant sound and in no time at all the path stops at the ocean. You sit for a while as you watch the waves crashing upon the beach. Feel the enchantment of this place.

You hear a rustle behind you and you turn to see a mother emu with her six baby chicks. She is saying hello and asking if you would like to come back to her nest for dinner and to spend the night. You excitedly say, "Yes, that would be so exciting." So you follow the mother emu back to her nest in the bush.

When you get back to her nest, you meet the chicks' father. He is very kind. Take a deep breath as you sit down for dinner. Their father has been preparing dinner while you have been cuddling the baby emus. There are nuts, flowers, fried caterpillars, grasshoppers and leaves with some fly soup to finish off with for dinner. Give a blessing for the food you are about to eat tonight.

When you have eaten your dinner, you all go to sleep on beds of flattened grass and leaves and fall into a deep sleep dreaming about the wonderful day you have had.

Dream peacefully with the family of emus. Feel the love from the emu family drift into your soul. Feel peace inside your heart. You are very safe. You are loved.

JESSI

THE END

HOW TO CREATE YOUR OWN MEDITATIONS

Maybe you would like to write some meditations yourself. It's very easy! All you have to do is find a quiet spot, relax and tell yourself you CAN do it! Let your mind be free.

You must be in a happy mood to write a meditation. There is just no point in writing a meditation when you are in a grumpy mood because all that will come out on your paper will be negative or unhappy feelings. Make sure you WANT to be writing the meditations. It is essential to let your mind be peaceful.

If you want to write a meditation we suggest you meditate before you actually write one, otherwise take a deep breath. It will be easier if you have silence when you write your meditation.

Before writing a meditation we suggest you lie down, close your eyes and allow your mind to be peaceful. Allow any thoughts to pass through your head. Drift for a while. When you feel you are ready, slowly open your eyes and then write whatever you feel. Be free to write anything at all. Don't worry about any grammar, punctuation or spelling as this can be corrected later. This is just the first draft.

Just remember, meditations need to be relaxing and peaceful, with no harm in them. The aim is to create a meditation that gives a sense of peace, security and love. You want to avoid anyone feeling fearful during your meditations. Try to bring a sense of serenity to the listener. Allow your energy and love to flow through your meditations and out into the world. You will learn and grow as you go. The most important thing is to ...

* * * ENJOY! * * *

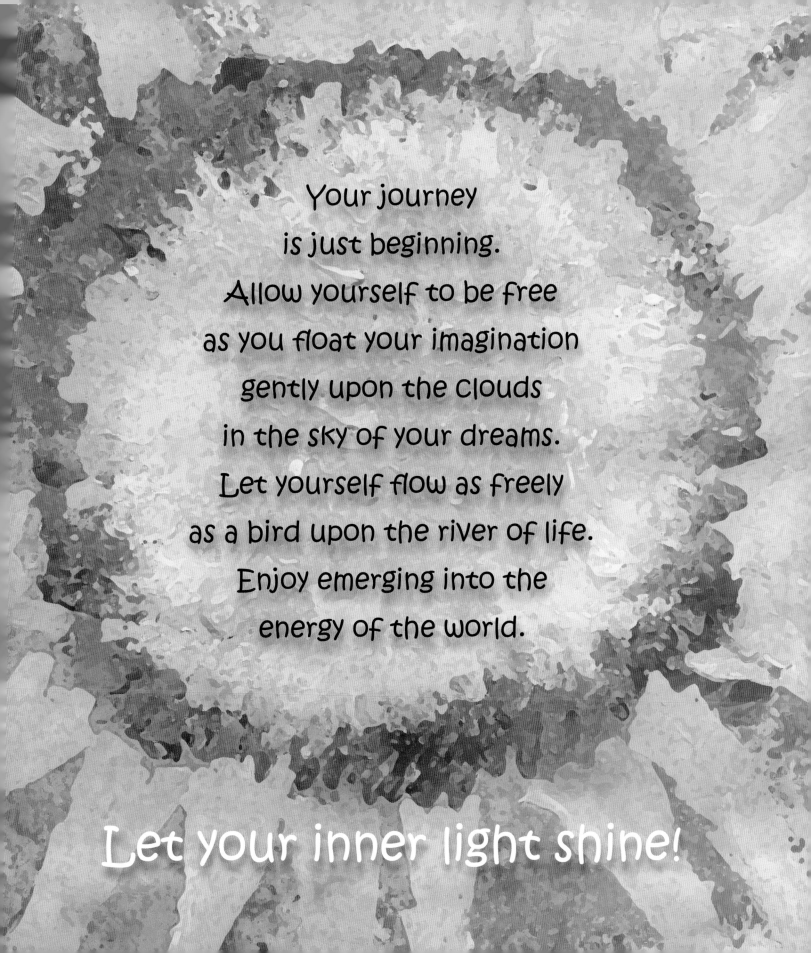

Your journey
is just beginning.
Allow yourself to be free
as you float your imagination
gently upon the clouds
in the sky of your dreams.
Let yourself flow as freely
as a bird upon the river of life.
Enjoy emerging into the
energy of the world.

Let your inner light shine!

G R A T I T U D E

We would like to thank the many people who helped us pull together our book by giving us encouragement and positive energy, which inspired us to manifest our dream of creating this meditation book. We have gained much enthusiasm from everyone surrounding us. They have offered just so much!

Thank you to our special extended family and all our friends who have tried out our meditations and read them, such as our precious Grandma, Joyce.

We give many thanks to our good friend Ian Cuming who has read our book and helped us by giving comments, time and energy.

A special thanks to our friend Richard Cooke from Raw Spirit Studios for his invaluable expertise, advice and encouragement … this book could not have happened without you.

We thank Andrew Barraclough from Morningside Printers for opening a doorway for our book. You know what you have done! Thank you for putting in extra effort and believing in us.

The four of us give many more thanks from the depths of our hearts to our loving and supportive mother, Lynn Maree Wynne, who has dedicated all her time, willingness and energy to helping us whenever we feel inspired, which has sometimes been in the middle of the night! She has been there!!! We thank her ever so much.

We also thank our special father, Chris Wynne, who has happily read our book and made many positive comments. He has also dedicated much of his time to give us computer skills along the way. His energy has been so encouraging. His soul is in part of this book.

Thank you. Much love,

Jessica, Ky, Tahnaya and Jarrah

C O M M E N T S

A MESSAGE FROM OUR FATHER:

This book is powerful! Transformational. Let it's energy ripple out into the world. Sit back and immerse yourself in this experience.   Congratulations my little souls. You have let your light shine for all to see. Now take a deep breath and head off into the horizon on your adventure.
Create with it what you want.

CHRIS WYNNE

This book is an indescribable wealth of peace and security. It is able to calm troubled minds and curb negative feelings. It can open your heart and allow love to flow freely from within.
I personally benefited from this book. My feeling is that it will heal many people for many years to come.

ROSE HERBERT – AGE 12

I absolutely love this book! It offers such a rich mix of images, feelings and ideas. It instructs me in the way of meditation and guides me to a place in myself that is nurturing and restorative.
This is the third time I have read from it and cried. Thank you Jessi, Ky, Tahnaya and Jarrah.

IAN CUMING – ARTISTIC DIRECTOR, COMMUNITY CULTURAL DEVELOPMENT WORKER,
EDUCATOR, PUPPETRY AND THEATRE SPECIALIST

Thanks for letting me be part of your special journey by reading "Meditations For Kids By Kids".
It made me remember dancing around the toadstool as a Moora Moora at Brownies. I snuggled my Koala Teddy in bed and felt very safe and loved….THANK YOU!

BRIDGET O'SHANNASSY – REIKI PRACTITIONER, RELAXATION THERAPIST, CHARITY WORKER

Everyone should take 'time out' of their busy life to read your book quietly and alone to explore relaxation with meditation. Continue to share your inner 'sparkling star' with love through your adventures and journeys of life.

An inspiration, Well Done!

KAREN STEINMAN – MOTHER

In this beautiful book we see an incredible creativity and use of language. For children so young I am amazed at the Wynne children's connection with 'self', their appreciation and knowledge of nature and their unique way of finding beauty in the world. The children have a deep understanding about what really matters in life, something that many of us take an entire lifetime to learn.

These words and pictures will take children away from the rush, bustle and harsh realities of the world, opening up a world full of imagination that is endless, safe and full of love. It will encourage them to connect with their feelings, release their fears and worries and provide them with some coping strategies in these days where beauty and innocence are so often forgotten.

HELEN SCHWIEGER – PRE-SCHOOL TEACHER

Your book reminded me that there is limitless space inside us (as well as outside). I love the way you throw your fears and worries up a tree or sadness into water. Your book shows that, as well as finding feelings and pictures in our minds and bodies that we have not chosen, we can choose to find more love, beauty, fun, cuddles or whatever we want. I wish I'd seen your book when I was a kid!

DAVID MACKAY – COUNSELLOR, PSYCHOLOGIST

MEDITATIONS FOR CHILDREN CD
BY ELIZABETH BEYER & TONI CARMINE SALERNO

For relaxation and imagination!

Help your children to enter the world of their imagination through these inspiring creative visualisations. Designed for primary school-aged children, these guided meditations will help kids tap into the magical world of their creativity and spirit.

For use during the day or at night, this series of meditations will calm and relax as Elizabeth and Toni's gentle and reassuring voices take them into their imaginations - where all is possible!

7 tracks / Approx. running time: 48 mins

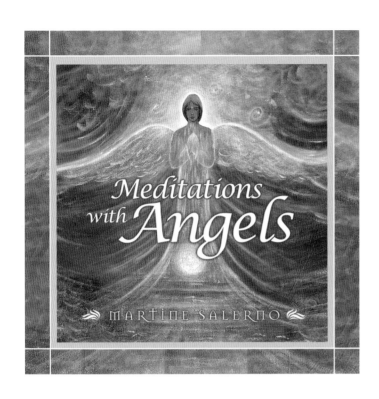

MEDITATIONS WITH ANGELS CD

BY MARTINE SALERNO

Connect with the Angelic Realm, through this heartfelt and energising series of meditations guided by Reiki Master Teacher Martine Salerno.

Accompanied by beautiful and healing music, 'Meditations With Angels' is a program you will want to use again and again.

You will be gently guided to experience and feel for yourself the all-encompassing love of the Angels surrounding you!

6 tracks / Approx. running time: 78 mins

TONI CARMINE SALERNO: MEDITATIONS FOR INNER PEACE CD

BY TONI CARMINE SALERNO

This inspiring series of guided meditations, composed and spoken by best-selling artist and author Toni Carmine Salerno will help calm the mind and create inner peace.

4 tracks / Approx. running time: 74 mins

GUARDIAN ANGEL CARDS

BY TONI CARMINE SALERNO

Guardian Angels are messengers of light.
They are here to lovingly guide you along life's Sacred Journey.
Receive daily inspiration, guidance and healing from your Guardian Angels through this beautiful card set.

Features 46 heart-shaped cards packaged in a hard-cover box.

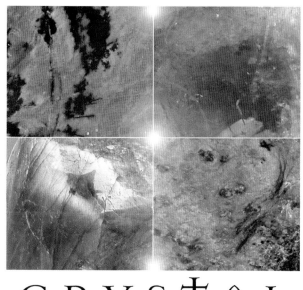

CRYSTAL ORACLE

BY TONI CARMINE SALERNO

Guidance from the heart of the Earth.

This beautifully presented set of 44 guidance cards featuring stunning photographs of crystals, gems and minerals plus an easy-to-use guidebook offers emotional support and practical guidance for everyday life.
'Crystal Oracle' is designed to inspire and heal you as you connect to the profound love and wisdom which stems from the heart of the Earth!

Features 44 cards and 88-page guidebook packaged in a hard-cover box.

For more information on any Blue Angel Gallery release,
please visit our website at:

www.tonicarminesalerno.com